ANDY'S GONE WITH CATTLE

For the Aged P's

© Illustrations JOHN ANTHONY KING

First published 1984 by William Collins Pty Ltd, Sydney
First published in paperback 1986
Typeset by Savage Type Pty Ltd Brisbane
Printed by Dai Nippon Printing Co (Hong Kong) Ltd

National Library of Australia
Cataloguing-in-Publication Data

   Lawson, Henry, 1867–1922.
     Andy's gone with cattle.

     For children.
     ISBN 0 00 184317 6.

     1. Ballads, Australian — Juvenile literature.
     I. King, J. A. (John Anthony), 1949–. II. Title.

A821'.044

ANDY'S GONE WITH CATTLE

Poem by Henry Lawson
Illustrations by John Anthony King

FONTANA PICTURE LIONS
Collins Australia

Our Andy's gone with cattle now —

Our hearts are out of order —

With drought he's gone to battle now
Across the Queensland border.

He's left us in dejection now,
Our thoughts with him are roving;

It's dull on this selection now,
Since Andy went a-droving.

Who now shall wear the cheerful face
In times when things are slackest?

And who shall whistle round the place
When Fortune frowns her blackest?

Oh, who shall cheek the squatter now
When he comes round us snarling?

His tongue is growing hotter now
Since Andy crossed the Darling.

Oh, may the showers in torrents fall,

And all the tanks run over;

And may the grass grow green and tall
In pathways of the drover;

And may good angels send the rain
On desert stretches sandy;

And when the summer comes again
God grant 'twill bring us Andy.